# The Easter Book

Macdonald

# Contents

# Celebrating Spring

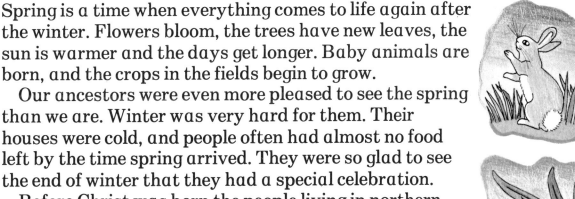

Spring is a time when everything comes to life again after the winter. Flowers bloom, the trees have new leaves, the sun is warmer and the days get longer. Baby animals are born, and the crops in the fields begin to grow.

Our ancestors were even more pleased to see the spring than we are. Winter was very hard for them. Their houses were cold, and people often had almost no food left by the time spring arrived. They were so glad to see the end of winter that they had a special celebration.

Before Christ was born the people living in northern Europe had a goddess called Eostre, the goddess of spring. Every year, in spring the people had a festival for her. The name of our spring festival, Easter, comes from the name Eostre.

We still keep some customs from that time. For example, in those days people cooked special cakes for the festival, rather like hot cross buns of today.

The Easter we know is a Christian festival. It is a time when people remember the story of how Jesus was killed, and rose again from the dead. This happened in spring, so Christians celebrate at this time of year.

Since then, many spring celebrations have become part of Easter. The Greeks and many other people in the ancient world kept religious customs in spring. When they became Christians, they carried on with these making them into Easter traditions which they still keep, such as lighting special fires and candles.

Eggs are a special symbol of Easter in many countries of the world. It is easy to see why. An egg hatches into a baby bird, so it makes a symbol for the new life that comes to the world at spring time.

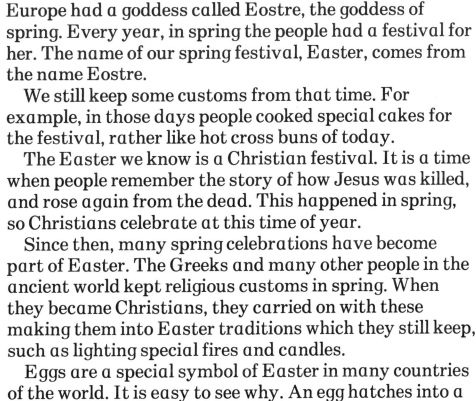

# Eggs for Easter

The custom of giving eggs at Easter is very old. The first Easter eggs were just ordinary hard boiled eggs, painted or dyed. In some places in the north of England this is still done.

In Germany, there is a tradition that green eggs are eaten on the Thursday before Easter. The people dye the eggs by boiling them with spinach.

In Greece, people used to dye eggs red for Easter, but now they dye them all colours. The eggs are used in a special Easter greeting. Each person carries an egg, and when two people meet they knock the eggs together, saying 'Christ is risen.'

In some countries, children play a game, a bit like conkers, using hard boiled eggs. They use painted eggs. Two players each hold an egg in their right hand, and knock the pointed ends together. The idea of the game is to crack the other person's egg first. The winner is the person whose egg has cracked the most others, but has not cracked itself.

Egg rolling is another old Easter game. Children roll eggs down a grassy slope. They do it to see whose gets to the bottom first, or to try to hit other eggs.

In Britain, the most famous egg rolling is in Preston in Lancashire. In America, an egg rolling competition is held every year on the lawn of the President's house, the White House in Washington.

In many countries, the children get up very early on Easter day and hunt for eggs, which their parents have hidden in the house and garden. The eggs are usually chocolate, but they used to be dyed or painted.

Sometimes the children make a special nest in the garden for the eggs. There is a story that the Easter Hare comes in the night and leaves the Easter eggs. He is sometimes called the Easter Bunny.

In many countries, roast lamb is eaten as a special Easter meal. In Greece, the lamb is roasted on a spit, and the Italians make a salad with hard boiled eggs to eat with it.

There are many different kinds of Easter cakes too, especially in Italy and Germany. There are some recipes for Easter food on pages 20 and 21 of this book.

Egg knocking game

Greek cake
with a
dyed egg

Decorated eggs

# Egg Craft

You might like to make your own decorated eggs for Easter. Here are some ideas. You should use hard boiled eggs for most of them. If you want to eat the eggs later, use vegetable dyes like onion or beetroot. Do not varnish eggs you want to eat. You can make them shine by rubbing them with a little vegetable oil.

You can make a hollow egg by blowing the inside out. To do this you must use an egg that has been in a warm room for a few hours, and not one that has just come out of the refrigerator and is very cold.

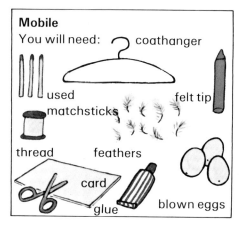

**Mobile**
You will need: coathanger
used matchsticks
felt tip
thread    feathers
card
glue    blown eggs

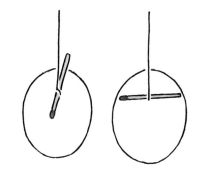

Tie a match to a thread and put it inside an egg.

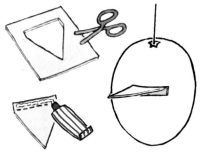

Cut out a beak shape. Fold and glue it, as the picture shows. Stick it on to the egg, like this.

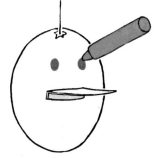

Draw in the eyes with a felt tip pen. Make them big.

Glue two feathers on to each egg. These make the wings.

Hang the birds from the coathanger. Make sure they balance nicely.

## How to blow an egg

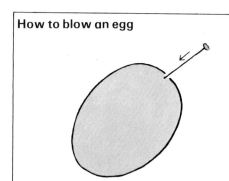

Prick the big end with a pin.

Make the hole bigger by chipping away the shell.

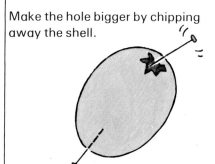

Make a hole in the small end. Put your fingers over each hole and shake the egg hard to break the yolk.

Blow through the small hole and empty the egg into a bowl.

Let the shell dry out.

Remember! The eggs must be room temperature, or you will not be able to blow them.

## Dyes

spinach

onion

beetroot

tea

vinegar (for fixing)

Boil the onion skin for half an hour.

Sieve the skins and let the water cool. Put the eggs in and boil them until they are a good colour. Add a few drops of vinegar, to fix the dye.

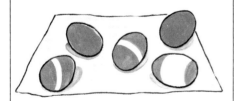

Drain and dry the eggs.

You can make the eggs patterned by using masking tape before you dye them.

## Wax-pattern egg
You will need:

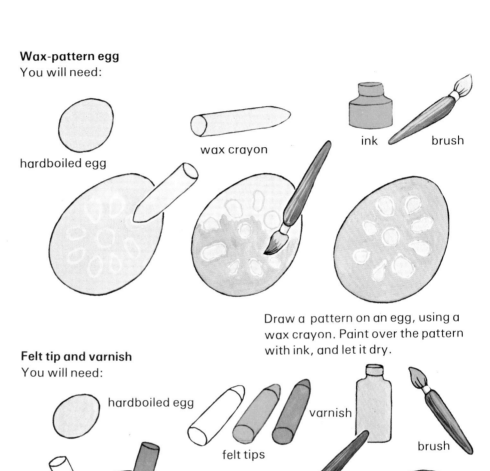

hardboiled egg

wax crayon

ink

brush

Draw a pattern on an egg, using a wax crayon. Paint over the pattern with ink, and let it dry.

## Felt tip and varnish
You will need:

hardboiled egg

felt tips

varnish

brush

Draw a picture, and then varnish the egg. Do the top part first. Let it dry, and then do the bottom half.

## Criss-cross egg
You will need:

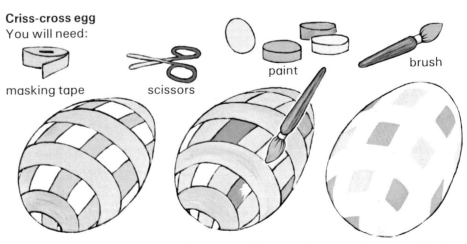

masking tape

scissors

paint

brush

Make a criss-cross pattern on the egg, using masking tape. Paint over it.

Remove the tape when the paint is dry, and you should have a pattern.

# Breaking the Ice at Easter

The winter has no pity
On a silent northern city,
   When you can't hear what is spoken
   And the words they say are frozen,
Falling solid from their lips.

But wait until it's Easter,
When it's warm, or when at least a
   Breath of air is not so bitter,
   And a thaw begins the pitter
And the patter of the drips.

For out run all the people,
And the bells rock every steeple,
   And the sun goes dancing higher
   As they light their Easter fire
To unfreeze their frozen lips.

**by Richard Blythe**

When Easter ends the winter,
Icy talk begins to splinter,
   And the lumpy words go runny;
   But it's not so very funny
To be deafened all to bits.

For silence turns to babble
As their words thaw out and gabble,
   From a patter to a clatter,
   Filling streets with melting chatter
From their winter's tales and quips.

Then springtime has no pity
On that noisy Easter city,
   For you can't hear what you utter
   When the place is all a-clutter
With what froze on winter's lips.

# Easter Presents

In Germany and Sweden and some other countries people decorate small branches and twigs at Easter.

In Germany, they use willow branches. They decorate these with ribbons, blown out painted eggs and pretzels, which are a kind of biscuit, made in a knot shape.

In Sweden, they use birch branches and decorate them with coloured feathers. The pictures show you how to do this. You must use inks to dye the feathers, as paint will not stick.

You may need help to cut the wire and to fix it tightly

**Nest of eggs**
You will need:

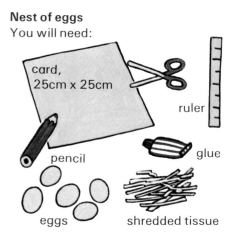

card, 25cm x 25cm, scissors, ruler, pencil, glue, eggs, shredded tissue

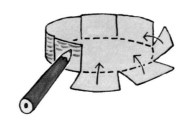

Draw two circles like these. Draw four lines through the centre to the edges. Cut them like this.

Fold the cut edges up like this and tape them together.
Decorate the outside of the basket.

Fill the basket with shredded tissue paper and put in Easter eggs.

---

**Giant papier maché egg**
You will need:

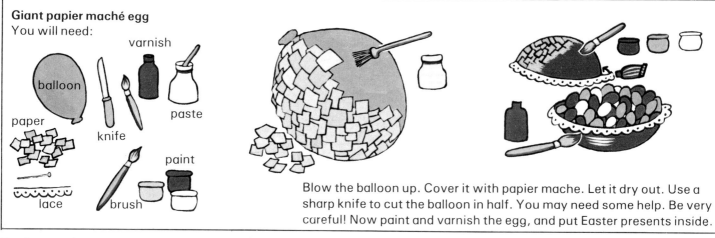

balloon, varnish, paper, knife, brush, paint, paste, lace

Blow the balloon up. Cover it with papier mache. Let it dry out. Use a sharp knife to cut the balloon in half. You may need some help. Be very careful! Now paint and varnish the egg, and put Easter presents inside.

---

**Donkey carrier**
You will need:

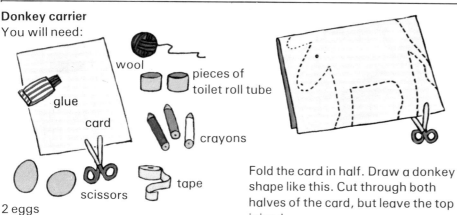

wool, pieces of toilet roll tube, glue, card, crayons, 2 eggs, scissors, tape

Fold the card in half. Draw a donkey shape like this. Cut through both halves of the card, but leave the top joined.

Join the two halves of the donkey's nose together, using glue. Do the same for the tail. Fix on the mane and the carriers, and put the eggs in.

## Birch twigs

**You will need:**

birch twigs

feathers

wire

inks

wire cutters

on to the twig without cutting into the stem.

Use a twig with buds on it, which you can pick and decorate a few days before Easter. Put it in water and wait for the leaves to come out.

Most of the things on this page are easy to make. You may need some help with the giant Easter egg, if you want to cut it in half. Ask a grown-up to do this, using a very sharp knife.

Line it with a paper doilly or a piece of fabric and put sweets, or an Easter present inside.

Dye the feathers different colours, using inks. Let them dry out.

Fix the feathers to the twigs, using wire and wire cutters.

Put the twigs in water for a few days. Soon the leaves will come out.

## Bunny basket

**You will need:**

2 squares of card, 20cm x 20cm

paper pins

ruler

glue

felt tipped pens

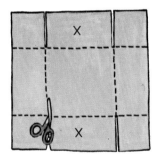

Cut the square in four places. Fold along the dotted lines and make X marks as the picture shows.

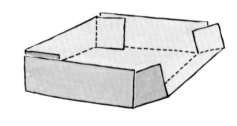

Fold up the sides to make the basket. Stick the corner flaps inside the walls of the basket.

Fold the other card in half and draw a rabbit shape like this. Cut it out.

Fix a rabbit over each X mark. Join the rabbits at the ears. Stick a cotton wool tail on, over the pin.

Fill the bunny basket with tissue paper and put in the eggs. This makes a good Easter present.

# Easter Bonnets

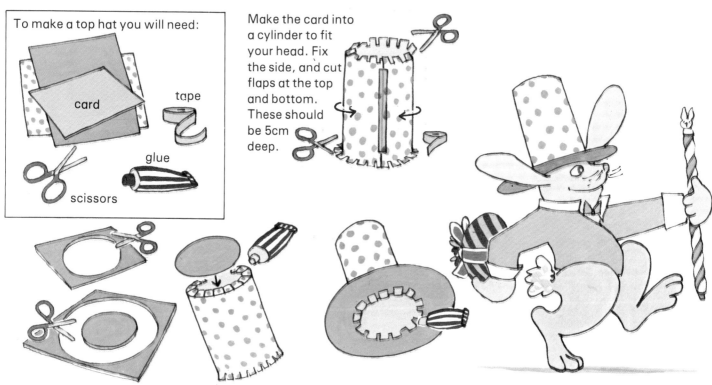

To make a top hat you will need:

card
tape
glue
scissors

Make the card into a cylinder to fit your head. Fix the side, and cut flaps at the top and bottom. These should be 5cm deep.

Make a brim. Cut a hole in the brim for your head. Use the cylinder as a template to get the size right.

Cut a top for the hat. Use the cylinder you have made as a template. Fix the top on with glue.

Push the hat through the hole. Glue the brim on, and decorate your hat.

In some towns and cities there is a big parade on Easter Sunday, with an Easter bonnet competition when people wear funny hats. These are often ones they have made themselves.

The idea comes from the time when it was the custom to wear new clothes on Easter day.

One of the most famous Easter Parades is in a place called Atlantic City in America. Here, they have a competition to decide which people are the best dressed.

There is a big Easter Parade in London too, and in many other places.

Perhaps you could arrange an Easter Parade and a bonnet competition with your friends.

See if you can make an Easter hat for yourself. The pictures show you how to make the shapes for a bonnet, or a hat, but the decorations are up to you.

Or you could make something quite different. There is a story that a lady once turned up at an Easter Parade wearing a hat just like a birdcage, with real birds in it!

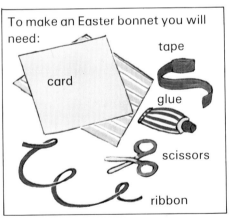

To make an Easter bonnet you will need:

card
tape
glue
scissors
ribbon

Bend the card like this to make a brim and cut flaps 5cm deep.

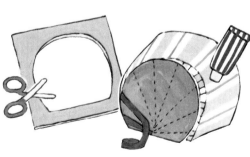

Cut out the bonnet back and fit it on to the brim. Stick the flaps on the inside.

Fix the ribbons on with glue and decorate your hat.

Now you are ready for Easter Parade. Good luck!

# Fun and Games

**Find the pairs of eggs**

## Rabbits and eggs
### A game for four players

Put your home made counters face down and mix them up. Put them on the rabbit squares at the bottom of the page, still face down.

The aim of the game is to get all the coloured rabbit counters to the same coloured eggs at the top of the page, with one counter on each egg.

Each player throws a dice. The person with the highest score chooses a colour and turns over the rabbits opposite it. The next highest scorer chooses another colour and so on.

Now the game starts. Players take turns to throw the dice and move a counter of their chosen colour, one square at a time, in any direction according to the number thrown. If one card lands on another, the one already there must go back to the start.

Get the Easter Bunny to the Easter eggs

## Egg blowing game

This is a game that people play on Easter Sunday in Germany. You need a blown egg. Look at page 8 to see how to make one.

The players must stand around the table and blow the egg to one other. They must not let it fall off the table.

# Rabbits and Eggs

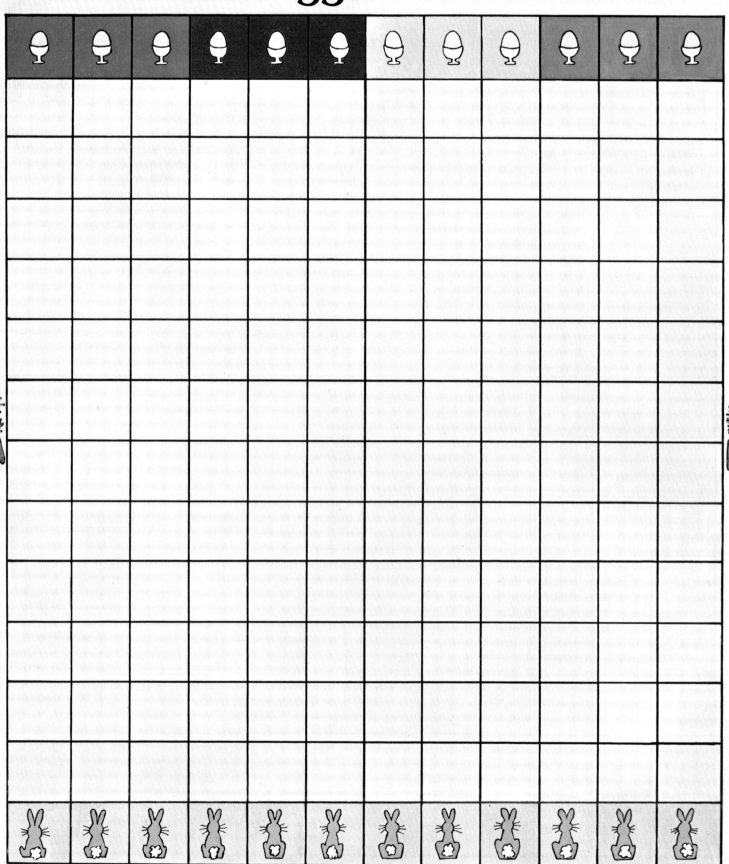

Make 12 counters, using thin card. Make them the right size to fit on the squares. The cards should all look the same on one side.

Draw a rabbit on the other side. Use four colours, so that you have three rabbits in each colour.

# The Easter Hare

Tom and Joanna liked having afternoon tea at Gran's. They used to go to her house every Thursday after school. They drank tea out of pretty china cups and ate scones with strawberry jam and big dollops of thick cream.

When the weather was cold and grey they sat inside, all cosy and warm, and toasted their toes in front of the flickery flames of a roaring log fire. When the weather was fine and sunny they sat out in the garden.

Gran and children played a game. They took it in turns to tell a story every week. The children always thought that Gran's stories were the best.

The Thursday before Easter, Tom and Joanna were on holiday from school. This Thursday had a special name. It was called Maundy Thursday. The children helped their mother and father on the farm most of the day. They collected the hens' eggs and cleaned out the rabbits' hutch and fed the pigs.

At half past three they changed into clean clothes and brushed their hair. It was time to go to Gran's. Mum had been busy in the farmhouse kitchen baking a fruit cake. It was an Easter present for Gran. She put it in a basket and gave it to the children to carry between them.

There was a large field between the farm and village of Honeysuckle Hill where Gran lived. The children climbed a stile to get into the field, and set off across the grass.

It was a lovely afternoon for a walk. The sky was blue, and the weather was very warm for April. A very gentle breeze ruffled the new leaves on the trees. Dad's milking

cows were grazing on the grass. They lifted their heads and gazed at the children with their soft brown eyes.

Suddenly, Tom stopped and pointed ahead. 'Look,' he whispered, 'there, near that mound of earth.' Joanna shielded her eyes from the sun and looked. It was the biggest hare she had ever seen. It sat quite still on its haunches, watching them. Its ears were enormous, and stood straight up on top of its head. The children could just see its long whiskers.

Tom and Joanna walked forward with the basket dangling between them.
'It's sure to run away now,' said Tom. But it did not move a step. It stayed in exactly the same place and stared at them. The children went closer and closer. The hare sat there.

'This is weird,' said Joanna when they were only a few paces away. 'Hares always run away when somebody comes.'

'Perhaps it's a special sort of hare,' replied Tom.

No sooner had he said this, than the hare bounded away. It reached a copse on the edge of the field and stopped. It turned and looked back at them.

When Tom and Joanna got to Gran's cottage they burst in the front door. 'Guess what! We've just seen the hugest hare in the world and it didn't run away from us, not even when we went right up close to it,' gabbled Tom all in one breath.

'My goodness!' exclaimed Gran, taking the basket from them. 'Well you had better come and tell me all about it. The tea and scones are ready, and we have Mum's nice cake to eat too.'

Tom and Joanna helped Gran to set out the tea things.
Gran poured the tea while the children told her about the hare and helped themselves to scones and cake.

'Well fancy that!' said Gran. 'It must have been the Easter Hare.' Her eyes twinkled.

Tom looked puzzled. 'What's the

**by Liz Cooper**

Easter Hare?' he asked.

'I shall tell you about him,' Gran replied. 'It's my turn for the story this week isn't it?'

The children nodded.

They listened while Gran told her story. It was about her when she was a little girl. Her mother had told her that if she made a nest for the Easter Hare, it would come on Easter Day and leave some chocolate eggs for her. So she had gone into the garden and built a nest out of leaves and twigs and moss. Sure enough, there were eggs in it on Easter day. They were made of chocolate and wrapped in gold paper.

On the way home from Gran's, Tom and Joanna decided that they would try making a nest for the Easter Hare too.

'I think we should make the nest tomorrow morning after breakfast,' said Tom.

Joanna agreed. 'Yes,' she said. 'Then it will be ready in plenty of time for the Easter Hare to come and leave his eggs on Sunday.'

The next day was Good Friday. Tom and Joanna had their breakfast early and went out into the farmyard.

'It will need to be quite a big nest for a hare, won't it?' said Joanna.

'Yes, it will,' said Tom.

They collected a pile of twigs and leaves and moss, just as Gran had said, and put them on a large piece of light wire mesh. Then they wrapped the mesh around to make the shape of a nest with a hollow in the middle. To make a lining they got handfuls of mud and packed it over the wire mesh, smoothing it with their hands.

A few hours later, the mud was dry, and Tom and Joanna scattered some soft, downy duck feathers inside the nest. Dad stopped to have a look on his way from the tractor shed to the house. 'That's a fine nest,' he said. 'Who's it for?'

'The Easter Hare,' said Tom proudly.

'Oh, I see,' said Dad. 'Where are you going to put it?'

'Over there by the stile so that it's easy for the Easter Hare to find,' replied Joanna. 'We saw him yesterday. He lives in the field where the cows are.'

'Oh, does he indeed,' said Dad. 'I shall look forward to meeting him on Easter Day then.'

Dad walked on up to the house. The children picked up the nest carefully and moved it to the stile. They put it a little to one side so that no one would tread on it and settled it in a patch of long, thick grass.

On Saturday they checked it. It was still in the same place and quite safe.

It seemed years until Sunday morning.

At last it came. The children had to have their breakfast before they could go outside. Tom was so excited that he could only eat half a piece of toast, and hardly that.

At nine o'clock they rushed out into the farmyard and down to the Stile. As they came around the corner of the chicken sheds they scarcely dared to look.

When they did, they stopped and stared.

They could hardly see the nest.

Sitting in it was their biggest laying hen, Penelope. She sat like a queen. Her head was held high and her feathers were fluffed up all around her.

'Penelope!' shouted Tom, crossly. 'Get off. That's the Easter Hare's nest.'

Poor Penelope squawked and flapped and flew away.

'Well, we'll have to come back later,' said Tom, heaving a big sigh.

'No we won't,' said Joanna. 'Look.' In the nest were five eggs. One of them was Penelope's. The other four were wrapped in shiny gold paper. There was a note with them. It said: 'HAPPY EASTER from the Easter Hare'.

The children jumped up on the stile and looked over into the field. An animal shot out of the long grass and raced across the field. Could it have been the Easter Hare—watching?

# Recipes

### Easter biscuits

You will need:

Oven electric, 180°C, 350°F,
gas mark 4.

1 beaten egg
A little lemon juice and grated lemon rind
225 grams self-raising flour
115 grams butter or margarine
115 grams sugar
50 grams currants
A pinch of salt

Mix the flour and the salt together. Rub in the fat, using the tips of your fingers. When it looks like breadcrumbs, add the sugar, the lemon rind, a teaspoon of lemon juice, and the beaten egg. Stir it all up then press it with your hands to make dough. Roll it out until it is about a centimetre thick and then cut it into shapes. You can use a cutter, or a rabbit template. Put the biscuits on a greased baking tray and cook them for 14 minutes in a warm oven. This makes 25-30 biscuits.

### Hot cross buns

You will need:

Oven electric, 220°C, 425°F
gas mark 4.

10 grams yeast (or one level desertspoon of dried yeast)
60 grams sugar, plus a teaspoonful for the yeast
1 teaspoon mixed spice and 1 of salt
¼ litre warm milk
450 grams plain flour
25 grams lard
60 grams sultanas

You will also need to make a glaze by mixing two tablespoons of sugar with two of water and boiling them up. Do this when the buns are nearly ready, as you must put the hot glaze on after they are cooked.

Add the teaspoonful of sugar to the milk. Stir it up, add the yeast. If you are using fresh yeast, crumble it first. If you use dried yeast, stir it into the milk for a few seconds using a whisk. Make sure the milk is warm, but not hot. If yeast gets too hot it does not work. Sprinkle a little flour on top of the milk and yeast mixture, and put it in a warm place for about 15 minutes, until it starts to look frothy. Again, do not let it get too hot.

Now turn the oven on. Put the rest of the flour in a warm bowl, mix the salt in and rub in the lard. Then put in the 60 grams of sugar, the sultanas and the mixed spice. Mix in the yeast and milk mixture to make a dough. You may need to add more milk.

Knead the dough well. This means you must push and stretch it on a floured board, roll it up and push and stretch it again. Do this for five or ten minutes.

Now roll it into a ball, cover it, and leave it for about 40 minutes, to rise. When it is twice the size it was, cut it into 12 pieces and gently shape each one into a bun. Put the buns on a greased tray, and use a knife to make the crosses.

Put them in the oven for about 20 minutes. Take them out and tap one on the bottom. If it sounds hollow, it is cooked. If not, put all the buns back for a few minutes. Paint the glaze on to the buns while they are hot.

## Italian Easter dove cake

You need some pieces of sponge cake large enough to cut into two dove shapes. You can make these using a sponge cake mix.
You will also need to make a dove shape template like the one in the picture. Use this to help cut the sponge cake.

You will also need:
1 carton whipping cream, sweetened
Fruit flavoured syrup (used for putting on ice creams)
The white of an egg and some water
250 grams of icing sugar
Whip the cream until it is stiff. Spread it over one dove shape, and put the other on top. Put the egg white into a bowl, beat it with a fork and add icing sugar, a spoonful at a time. Before it gets stiff, add about three spoons of water, and enough syrup to make the mixture change colour. Go on adding icing sugar until the mixture is nearly stiff then spread it over the top of the dove cake.

**The story of the dove cake**

Once, in Italy, there was a king who wanted to capture a city.

But his horse did not agree with him and would not gallop to battle.

The horse changed his mind when a girl offered him a cake like a dove, the bird of peace. Then the king changed his mind too, and decided not to conquer the city.

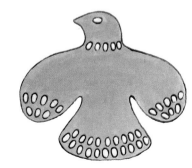

# Did You Know?

These pictures show some old Easter customs that are still kept. One of them is an odd game that is played every Easter Monday in Hallaton in Leicestershire.

First, big meat pies are baked. Slices are thrown to the villagers and everyone scrambles for a piece. Then there is a bottle kicking game against the next village, Medbourne. The 'bottles', which are used as footballs are three small beer kegs. Each team tries to get the bottles across a small stream that flows between the two villages. Afterwards, everyone drinks the beer.

Hare pie scrambling and bottle kicking are very old customs in the village of Hallaton in Leicestershire. The pies are not really made from hares, and the three bottles are small barrels. Two hold beer, and one is empty.

This strange sign can be seen in a village called Biddenden in Kent. The women are called the Biddenden maids. There is a story that Siamese twins, joined together at the head and the hip, lived in the village 800 years ago. When they died they left some land to the villagers. The wheat that was grown on the land was to be used to make flour for bread, and given to the poor. Big loaves of bread are still given out on Easter Monday.

**Springtime jokes**

Q Which side of the chicken had the most feathers?
A *The outside.*

Q How do you stop a cock crowing on Monday morning?
A *Eat him for Sunday lunch.*

Q What did the Spanish farmer say to his chicken?
A *Olé.*

Q Who came second after the hare when the animals had a race?
A *A hot cross bun!*

These huge statues can be found on Easter Island, in the Pacific Ocean. No one really knows how they got there, but many experts think that they were built hundreds of years ago by people who came from South America. The Island got its name because it was discovered by Dutch sailors at Easter time in 1722.

There is a pub in East London called the Widows Son. It is said to have been built on land where a widow's house once stood. The widow had a son who was a sailor. One Good Friday, when she was expecting her son to come home from sea, she baked him a hot cross bun. But he was shipwrecked. His mother always believed he would one day return and every year she baked another bun, but he never came back.

Every year the landlord of the pub asks a sailor to put a bun in a basket.

In Germany, there is a tradition that an egg laid on Good Friday will last for 100 years. But if you eat it at once it will make you very healthy.

Some people say that Good Friday is the best day for planting potatoes.

In Eastern Europe, there is tradition that it is good luck to sprinkle water on people at Easter time. These people have dressed up in traditional costume for the game.

# Spring Flowers

Try growing some bulbs this spring. The pictures show you how to grow them in a bowl indoors. This makes the bulbs flower sooner in the year than they would if they were outside. You may like to give them as a present on Mothering Sunday.

You can buy bulbs in the shops in autumn. Plant them in October or November, either indoors or out.

The first spring flowers are snowdrops and crocuses. Daffodils come later.

You could grow some spring flowers in a window box.

**Bulbs**
You will need:

bulbs

large bowl

bulb fibre

bucket

Put the fibre into the bucket. Fill the bucket with water and leave it overnight.

Next day, squeeze the water from the fibre and half fill the bowl.

Put the bulbs in the bowl.

Press them into the fibre and fill in the spaces with more squeezed fibre. Press it down firmly, but leave the tips showing.

Now put the bowl in a cupboard. It should be dark, but airy and cool. Leave the bulbs for two months. Keep the fibre moist, but not too wet.

Bring the bowl out into the warmth and sunlight. Keep the fibre moist, and soon the flowers will bloom.

Daffodils are bulbs.

Snowdrops are corms.

Crocuses are corms.

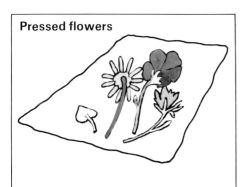

**Pressed flowers**

Put the flowers face down on blotting paper. Put another sheet on top.

Press the blotting paper and flowers with heavy books.

If you do that, you don't have to keep them in the dark. Just plant them outside, and when spring comes they will start to grow. You could grow polyanthus in the window-box. These are not bulbs but plants like primroses, and they come in many colours. It is easier to buy them from a garden shop as plants, not seeds.

If you want to press flowers, it is best to use some from a garden, or ones you have grown yourself. Don't use wild flowers as many of these are becoming rare. If too many people pick them, there will be none left.

**Daffodil**
You will need: card, egg carton, pinking shears, yellow paint and green pipe cleaner.

Cut the cup of an egg box with pinking shears. Paint it yellow and let it dry.

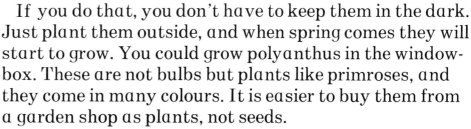

Cut the yellow card into petal shapes. Knot one end of the pipe cleaner and push it through the two bits of the flower, like this.

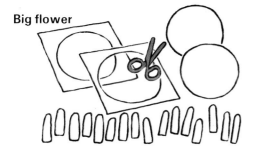

**Big flower**

Cut two circles the same size and make petals from card.

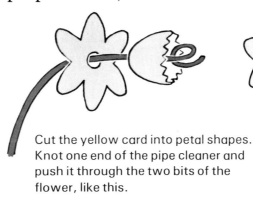

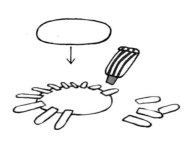

Stick the petals on to one circle, like this. Then stick the other circle on top.

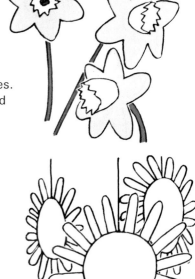

Hang the flowers from the ceiling, or use them to make a mobile.

# Late Summer Easter

In Australia, because the seasons are different, Easter comes at the end of summer instead of in spring.

The weather is still quite warm, and families like to go off to the country for a short holiday. The people in the picture are on a camping holiday.

In one of the biggest towns, Sydney, there is a big agricultural show called the Royal Easter Show. There are exhibitions of fruit and vegetables and home made jams.

There is also a cattle show, a special kind of horse racing, show jumping, a cat show, children's art

ROYAL EASTER SHOW

I AM AN ARTIST

competitions, a funfair and many other kinds of exhibitions. The children buy bags of goodies from the stalls, go on rides at the fair and watch firework displays.

Out in the country, the fruit is growing ripe, and many farmers are busy.

Some European traditions have been taken to Australia by the people who have gone to live there. One of these is the Easter Bunny. People hide eggs in the garden for the children to find, just as they do in Europe.

# Easter-time Poems

### Spring

Nothing is so beautiful as Spring —
   When weeds, in wheels, shoot long and lovely and
     lush;
   Thrush's eggs look like little low heavens, and thrush
Through the echoing timber does so rinse and wring
The ear, it strikes like lightnings to hear him sing;
   The glassy peartree leaves and blooms, they brush
   The descending blue; that blue is all in a rush
With richness; the racing lambs too have fair their fling

    Gerard Manley Hopkins

### The Donkey

When fishes flew and forests walked,
   And figs grew upon thorn,
Some moments when the moon was
     blood,
   Then surely I was born;

With monstrous head and sickening cry
   And ears like errant wings,
The devil's walking parody
   On all four-footed things.

The tattered outlaw of the earth,
   Of ancient crooked will;
Starve, scourge, deride me; I am dumb,
   I keep my secret still.

Fools! For I also had my hour;
   One far fierce hour and sweet;
There was a shout about my ears,
   And palms before my feet.

    G. K. Chesterton

# Easter Cards

Easter cards are fun to make. The traditional pictures are of rabbits, hares, chicks and flowers.

These pictures will give you some ideas, but there are many more you can try. Silver paper can be very pretty. You could make a mosaic from pieces of eggshell stuck on to card.

You can make a pop-up rabbit, like the chick. He can jump in and out of his burrow. Or he could be a hare, peeping over the grass.

Instead of using pressed flowers for a card, you could cut out pictures from magazines or seed catalogues. Cut out plenty, and stick them down in layers, so they make it look like a big bunch.

Try making a surprise card by sticking the bouquet inside the card and leaving the cover plain.

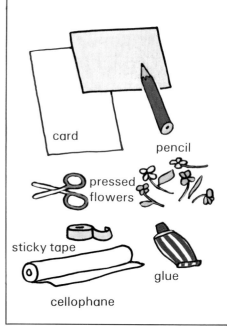

**Pressed flower card**
You will need:

card

pencil

pressed flowers

sticky tape

glue

cellophane

**Hatching chick card**
You will need:

These two pictures show the sort of cards people living in Germany about a hundred years ago sent to their friends.

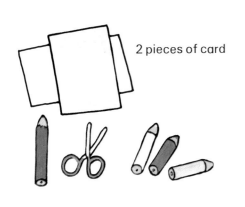

2 pieces of card

pencil    scissors    crayons

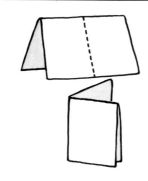

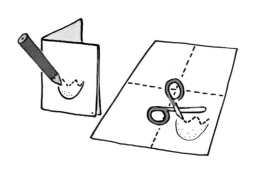

Fold a piece of card, like this, and draw half an egg shape on it. Cut along the zig-zag edge of the egg, as the picture shows. You might find it easier to cut out a whole egg shape, cut it in half, and stick one half on to the card.

28

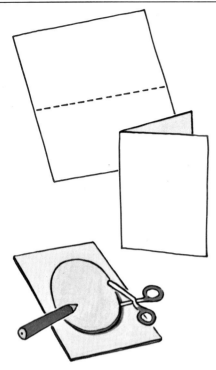

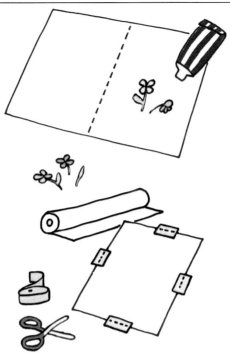

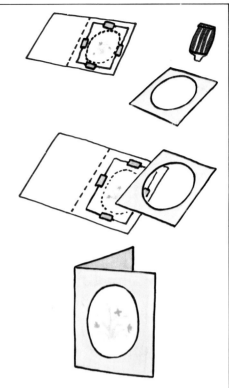

Fold the larger piece of card in half. Cut other piece to the same size as the front of the card, and carefully cut an oval from the centre.

Stick the pressed flowers in a pattern on the front of the card. Make sure the pattern will fit into the oval shape. Cover the flowers with cellophane, held in place with sticky tape.

Now stick the piece of card with the oval cut out over the cellophane. Fold the card again, and stand it up.

## Cotton tail card
You will need:

card

3 cotton wool tails

glue

crayons

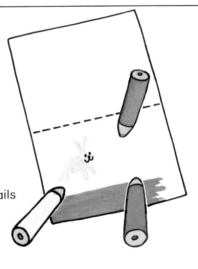

Draw a picture.

Stick on the tails.

Make a chick on a stalk like this. Stick a matching half of the egg on his head.

Push the chick through the slot in the front of the card.

Use the stalk as a lever to make the chick bob up and down.

# The Easter Story

This is the Christian Easter story.

Jesus lived almost two thousand years ago in a country called Judea. This land is now called Israel.

He preached a new kind of religion, and the leaders of the older religion thought he was dangerous, and might start a revolution.

One Sunday, Jesus rode into Jerusalem on the donkey. Crowds of people cheered him and called him king. Then he went into the temple, where, in those days, there were traders and money lenders. Jesus was very angry. He said that God's house was being made into a den of thieves. He tipped the stalls over and spilt the money everywhere.

His enemies were plotting to kill him, and they paid Judas, one of his friends to betray him.

It was the time of the Passover, and as Jesus was Jewish he wanted to celebrate this feast.

On the Thursday, his friends hired a room where they could eat the Passover meal with Jesus. Judas came to the meal, but left early.

Afterwards, Jesus went with his friends into a garden called Gethsemane. Soon Judas arrived with some armed men who took Jesus away.

First Jesus was tried by a religious court who said he had broken God's laws by calling himself the Son of God. The punishment for this was death, but no-one was allowed to kill him without permission from the Romans, who ruled the country.

So the next day Jesus was tried again by the Roman governor, Pontius Pilate, who would not interfere and allowed Jesus to be punished.

Then, Jesus was taken to a place called Golgotha and crucified. At the end of the day, when he was dead, his body was put in a tomb and a big stone rolled in front.

On the Sunday a woman called Mary Magdalene went to the tomb, only to find the stone had been rolled away, and the body of Jesus was gone. Two angels were there. They told her that Jesus had risen from the dead.

There are many stories of people seeing Jesus after he had risen from the dead. After this, Jesus' friends travelled about the world, preaching the new religion.